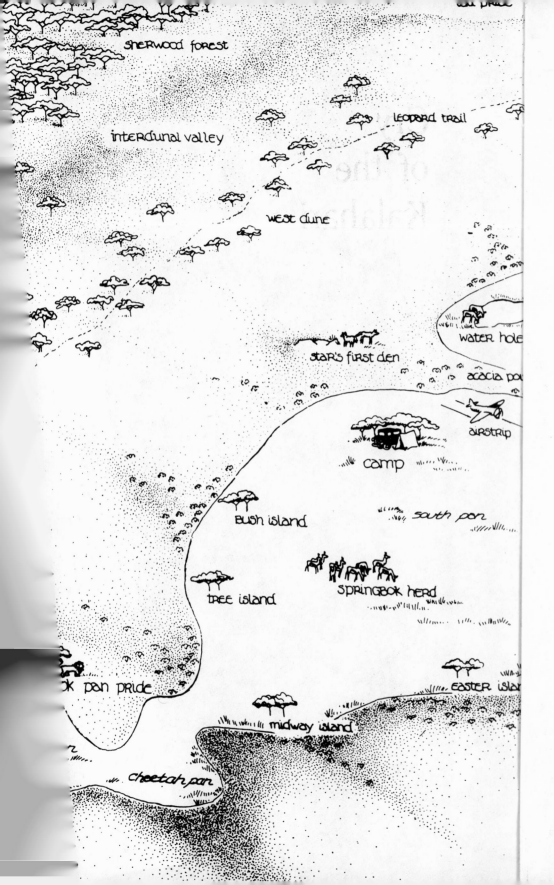

sherwood forest

interdunal valley

leopard trail

west dune

star's first den

water hole

acacia pou

airstrip

camp

bush island

south pan

tree island

SPRINGBOK HERD

k pan pride

EASTER islan

midway island

cheetah pan

Cry
of the
Kalahari

SPRINGB

springbok p

LORRAINE SNEE